Water Wise

By Myka-Lynne Sokoloff

CELEBRATION PRESS
Pearson Learning Group

Contents

Safety First!

Pools, lakes, beaches, and streams can all be a lot of fun. You may enjoy swimming or going boating. Maybe you prefer sitting on the beach and talking with friends. These activities are all great ways to enjoy the water.

Yet, each year people get hurt in and around water. That's why it's important to know about water safety. Following the rules while in and near water will keep you and others around you safe. If you are water wise, you'll stay safe and have lots of fun, too!

Safety Together

It's never a good idea to swim alone. If you get in trouble, there will be no one to get help. Always swim with a water partner. A water partner is someone who swims with you. This person stays near you and knows what you are doing. This way, if you are in trouble, your partner can get help. If your partner is not an adult, you must have an adult watch you in the water. The adult will be able to get help if needed.

Make sure an adult is nearby when you swim.

Beach Safety

There is nothing like a day at the beach. You can swim, ride the waves, or play in the sand. Remembering a few simple rules will keep you safe.

Wade or swim only in **designated** swimming areas, which are free of rocks, piers, and other dangers. These areas also allow the **lifeguard** to watch you. Lifeguards know how to save swimmers in danger. They also look out for dangerous **currents** and animals. That's why it's never a good idea to swim in an area without a lifeguard.

A lifeguard often sits in a high chair to watch people in the water.

(!) **Sun Protection**
Too much sun is bad for your skin. Be smart and always wear sunscreen, especially when you are in the water. A hat, shirt, and sunglasses will also help protect you.

It's important to read all signs and flags at the beach. Why? They will tell you if the water is safe. If you are not sure what a sign or flag means, ask a lifeguard or another adult. Listen for clues that there is danger. A lifeguard will blow his or her whistle when a swimmer is in trouble.

Signs and flags may not always tell you everything about the water. You should learn which animals live in and near the water and which ones to avoid. For example, you should not swim where there are **jellyfish**, sharks, or alligators.

Wearing beach shoes will protect your feet both in and out of the water.

ⓘ Check the Flags

Some flags look the same at most beaches. For example, a red flag alerts swimmers that the water is too rough to enter. A red and yellow flag means that there is a lifeguard on duty. Remember that different flags may be used at different beaches.

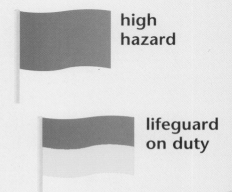

high
hazard

lifeguard
on duty

When you visit beaches, always make sure you understand what the local signs mean.

You still need to be careful even if you swim in a designated area. Strong currents can pull you away from the shore. If you are in a strong current, try not to panic. Alert your water partner, and call out to the lifeguard or another adult for help. If you are not a strong swimmer, do not try to swim back to the beach. Instead, swim **parallel** to the shore until you are out of the current. Then swim toward the beach.

Safety in Boats

Boating can be lots of fun. As with all water activities, the more you know, the safer you'll be. Some boats can tip easily. They can also move fast. Because of this, boats are sometimes dangerous. So, having an adult along is important.

You must wear a **life jacket** because it will help you float if you are in the water. Even if you are a good swimmer, you may get tired or the water may be very cold. A life jacket will keep your head above water until help arrives.

You can learn more about safety in boats by taking lessons with a trained instructor.

Always wear a life jacket when on the water.

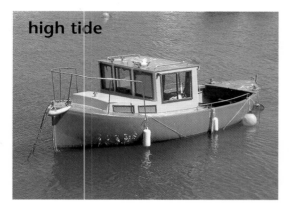

high tide

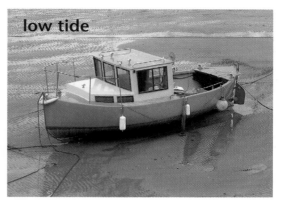

low tide

The boats in a harbor rise and fall with changes in the tide. The water is much deeper at high tide than at low tide.

Do not dive off a boat or a dock without first checking if the water is deep enough. The water levels are always changing due to the **tide**. Be sure to also follow the boating safety rules below. If you do, you'll stay safe and dry.

- Be careful getting into a boat. Squat down low, and keep your weight in the middle as you step into it.
- Never stand up in a small boat. It may tip over, or **capsize**.
- Always check weather reports to know if a storm is on the way.
- Never go out in a boat or swim during a thunderstorm. Lightning can be more dangerous on the water.
- Watch out for swimmers, other boats, and fishing lines.
- Always let someone know that you are going out in a boat and what time you expect to be home.

Safety at the Pool

People often forget to be careful at a swimming pool. Sometimes it seems less dangerous than the sea or a lake. It is very important to be water wise here, too. Remembering these few rules will help you stay safe at the pool.

- Walk, don't run, around a pool. The area around the pool is often hard, slippery, and dangerous.
- Know which is the deep end. Stay in the shallow area unless you are a very good swimmer.
- Never jump or dive into shallow water.
- Listen to the lifeguard or other adult watching you.
- Watch out for other swimmers and objects in the water.

You can use a kickboard to practice your swimming kicks.

Once you are a good swimmer, you can learn to dive.

Learn to Swim

One of the best ways to be water wise is to learn to swim. If you can swim well, you'll be much safer at the pool, beach, or river. Swimming is fun and is good exercise. You can enjoy other water sports like snorkeling, rowing, and water polo if you are a strong swimmer.

Always ask an adult to help you put on your mask and snorkel.

⊙ Emergency Plan

Follow these steps if someone falls in the water.

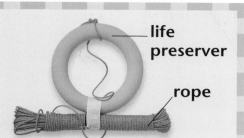

life preserver

rope

- ⊙ Call for help.
- ⊙ Toss a life preserver and use the rope to pull the person to safety.
- ⊙ Tell an adult immediately.
- ⊙ Call an emergency phone number for assistance.
- ⊙ Don't go into the water yourself unless you are trained in **lifesaving**.

telephone symbol

Even if you are a good swimmer, being careful is important. Know your limits when swimming into deep water. When swimming out from the shore, turn around and start back before you feel tired. If you need a rest, try floating on your back. Remember, don't be afraid to signal for help with a shout or a wave of your arms if you cannot make it to safety.

ⓘ Float to Safety

It is a good idea to learn basic lifesaving skills to be used in the water. Below are steps on how to make an emergency float with your pants. (If you are not wearing long pants, another piece of clothing may work.) Be sure to try this activity only with the help of an adult.

1. Remove your pants while you **tread water**. Knot the bottom of each leg.

2. Hold your pants behind you, with the waist open as wide as possible.

3. Fling the pants over your head so that air goes in. Do this again until the pants are filled with air.

4. Hold the waist closed with your hands. Rest your chin on the float. The float will keep you up.

Water Wrap-Up

Remember to be water wise, and make sure you learn as much as you can about water safety.

- Always swim and boat with an adult present.
- When in a boat, wear a life jacket at all times.
- Read all signs and obey rules.
- Learn to swim well.
- Don't swim where there are dangerous animals.
- Know what to do in the case of an emergency.

Goggles protect your eyes underwater.

Glossary

capsize   to turn or tip over

currents   flows of water in a certain direction

designated   set apart for a special purpose

jellyfish   a sea animal with a soft body and tentacles

lifeguard   someone who is trained to help swimmers in danger

life jacket   a jacket that will keep you floating if you fall into the water

lifesaving   having to do with the saving of human life

parallel   going in the same direction and being an equal distance apart

tide   the regular rise and fall of the ocean's surface about every 6 hours

tread water   to keep the body upright and head above water by moving the legs back and forth